The Little Book of
God's Big Promises

by Dr. Elizabeth Enns

Copyright ©2020 by Dr. Elizabeth Enns

To contact the author, please write to the below postal or email address:

Christians For Messiah Ministries
PO Box 36324
Rock Hill, SC 29732
Email: e.enns@antiochinternationalchurch.com

All scriptures taken from the New International Version unless otherwise noted. Scriptures taken from the Holy Bible, New International Version® ©2020.

All rights reserved. No part of this publication may be reproduced without prior permission of Christians for Messiah Publishing or Dr. Elizabeth Enns

First Christians for Messiah Publishing edition published 2020

Cover Design by: Rebecca Barrett

Editing by: Jesse Enns

Manufactured in the United States of America by Ingram Spark

ISBN: 978-1-7355929-0-9

Introduction

I used to be a classroom teacher and have worked with children for over twenty years. I learned very quickly that the days were consistently more successful when I arrived early, completely prepared and with a few extra supplies in the good old carpet bag, just in case. Life is like this. When we are prepared for the expected and ready for the surprises that arise, we find ourselves growing and even thriving through all sorts of seasons.

Today, you may experience a beautiful, peaceful day filled with wonderful moments. It may be full of love, peace and joy from the second that your feet hit the floor until the final hour when your head hits the pillow. But, on the other hand, you could have another sort of day. You could be faced with a wolf on the prowl seeking to make you his lunch, or a giant just looking to intimidate you and pick a fight. We don't need to cower in fear or hide, but we do need to be smart. Regardless of how our days unfold, we need to be prepared. We are at war, and although we have seasons where we find reprieve from some battles, we must be ready with the weapons that have been supplied and the wisdom and skills of how to use them effectively. So, I invite you to journey with me through God's word to discover the powerful weapons that are His promises.

"For no matter how many promises God has made, they are "Yes" in Christ. And so through him the "Amen" is spoken by us to the glory of God." (2 Cor.1:20 NIV) As new creations in Christ, we are called to partner with the Lord and stand on the truth of His promises. As we proclaim His Word, we open up the doors for supernatural breakthrough and living life abundantly.

About the Author

Dr. Elizabeth Enns comes from a long line of powerful Bible teachers. Her great grandfather, Derek Prince, is one of the foremost Bible scholars of the 20th Century. Following in the footsteps of those who have gone before her, Dr. Elizabeth Enns carries an anointing to bring revelation and passion to the people of God. She has her doctorate in Theology, and co-founded Antioch International Church, where she and her husband serve as senior pastors. They have three sons, and live together in the Carolinas. Elizabeth is also a certified school teacher. She brings all these experiences together to bring love, warmth, humor, revelation and the power of God through her ministry.

Dedication

To Ethan, Micah & Asher.
May you stand tall on the promises of God
and on the shoulders of the generations
who have gone before you.

The Little Book of God's Big Promises by Dr. Elizabeth Enns

My son, if you accept my words and store up my commands within you, turning your ear to wisdom and applying your heart to understanding—indeed, if you call out for insight and cry aloud for understanding, and if you look for it as for silver and search for it as for hidden treasure, then you will understand the fear of the Lord and find the knowledge of God.

Proverbs 2:1-5 (NIV)

The Little Book of God's Big Promises by Dr. Elizabeth Enns

Week 1

Making decisions is a constant in our life. Whether we enjoy making them and thrive as we do, or find it challenging and stressful, one thing is for sure – we all make them. Even the decision to not decide is in fact a decision. Laced within the process of life's more challenging decisions is the sometimes daunting question, "Is this the right choice?" God promises us throughout His Word that we can receive wisdom and understanding but these gifts come with a price. The Lord tells us here in Proverbs 2 that if we receive His words and commands and fill ourselves with them, and if we grow in His wisdom and apply it to our lives, we will receive this great promise: The Lord tells us that we will understand the fear of the Lord, which means that we will walk in the fear of the Lord and discover the knowledge of God.

So often we are desperate to know God's will so that we can walk in it and please Him. We get so consumed with the fear of making mistakes and wrong life choices that we forget this big promise. We forget this truth. We are His children and He loves each one of us so completely. His desire for us is to succeed and shine in wholeness for His glory. He promises us understanding and the knowledge required to walk in His ways. Be encouraged today that God is for you. He wants to give you wisdom and understanding, so that you can apply it to your life and grow in the confidence that you are walking in His ways each day.

The Little Book of God's Big Promises by Dr. Elizabeth Enns

The peace of God, which transcends all understanding, will guard your hearts and your minds in Christ Jesus.

Philippians 4:7 (NIV)

Week 2

Peace is something that we should never take for granted. When we can walk through each day with peace, no matter the storm that rages around us, then we have received a most valuable gift. When we become anxious and worried, that means that we are losing our peace. The Lord promises us that His peace will guard our hearts and minds, but if we are struggling with fear and anxiety, we have to ask ourselves why. *God's promises are true, so if we are suffering with this then we need to readjust our position.* Romans 14:17 tells us that the Kingdom of God is righteousness, peace and joy. So, if we are part of the Kingdom of God, we are supposed to walk in these three characteristics.

If we are not sticking close to the Father, then we can become discontent and disillusioned, and lose our joy. Once our joy is missing, it can be a challenge to celebrate with the Lord and we spend less time in His presence, so we start to lose our peace as fear and anxiety creep in. This is a dangerous place, because when we have lost our joy and our peace, that is when the enemy comes after our righteousness. This is not a mind over matter issue. This is a kingdom of God matter that can only be remedied by daily abiding in the vine. Be encouraged today to be Kingdom. Walk closely with the Lord and live in a place of joy, peace, and righteousness.

The Little Book of God's Big Promises by Dr. Elizabeth Enns

If my people, who are called by my name, will humble themselves and pray and seek my face and turn from their wicked ways, then I will hear from heaven, and I will forgive their sin and will heal their land.

2 Chronicles 7:14 (NIV)

The Little Book of God's Big Promises by Dr. Elizabeth Enns

Week 3

We are God's people, called by his name. We need to know who we are, and be thankful for it. As we choose to walk in humility and to be thankful in all situations, we open the door for this promise of the Lord to be released. Humility is something that is often misunderstood. It is not self-deprivation or a low self-esteem. Humility is an accurate understanding of who you are; it is the realization that without God and His gracious hand, you are nothing. It is Almighty God who makes us great, and it is His gifts that equip us for success on the journey. He gives us life and breath, and without Him we can do nothing. God gave you the skills and the motivation to hone your abilities and reach for the stars. He made a way for each one of us to succeed, and to boldly approach His throne. Through His son Jesus, He made us worthy. Apart from saying 'yes' and receiving salvation through His Son, there is nothing we can do, on our own, to be great. It's all His doing that makes us great. How humbling is that? So, I encourage you, in all humility, to be great for the glory of God and position yourself for greatness. In all things, seek Him and His ways, and walk closely with Him. Then, the promise of forgiveness and healing will be yours.

The Little Book of God's Big Promises by Dr. Elizabeth Enns

> Come to me, all you who
> are weary and burdened,
> and I will give you rest.

Matthew 11:28 (NIV)

The Little Book of God's Big Promises by Dr. Elizabeth Enns

Week 4

There are nights that when I finally climb into bed and exhale; I realize that I have carried an extra heavy load all day. As I welcome the presence of the Lord into my room, the realization of the weight that I was carrying becomes apparent. How often do we forget the promise of the Lord that offers us rest in moments like this? When we take our heavy burdens and exhaustion to the Lord, He lifts them off of us and replaces them with His peace. In His loving comfort, He blankets us and calms our thoughts and feelings. As I reflect on this promise I can't help but ask myself, 'Why don't I go to the Father earlier in the day?' I could give Him all my burdens as they arise and never carry them at all. Friends, I want to encourage you to recognize your burdens and heaviness as they arrive, and give them to our Father. He desires to carry them for us. Don't let them weigh you down; throw them off – He can catch.

The Little Book of God's Big Promises by Dr. Elizabeth Enns

Be strong and courageous.
Do not be afraid or terrified because of them, for the LORD your God goes with you; he will never leave you nor forsake you.

Deuteronomy 31:6 (NIV)

The Little Book of God's Big Promises by Dr. Elizabeth Enns

Week 5

Some days we can feel as though we face a world of giants alone. As the children of Israel approached the Promised Land, they were overcome with fear because of the giants they could see with their natural eye. As a result, they ended up missing out on what would have been one of the greatest triumphs. But after a forty year cooling off period, God gave them a second chance. They entered the land and took possession of all that God had promised them. I want to encourage you to stand on the promises of God today. Don't allow fear and unbelief to rob you of all that God has purposed for you. There are giants in the land but God has already shown us through the Israelites entering the Promised Land, and a small shepherd boy named David, that giants are no match for Him.

The Little Book of God's Big Promises by Dr. Elizabeth Enns

> But when you pray, go into your room, close the door and pray to your Father, who is unseen. Then your Father, who sees what is done in secret, will reward you.
>
> Matthew 6:6 (NIV)

The Little Book of God's Big Promises by Dr. Elizabeth Enns

Week 6

This journey with the Lord is all about our hearts, and developing a relationship with the Father. He is not looking for us to impress man with how spiritual we are, He is looking for us. When we share a personal relationship with the Father that is intimate and not public, then it affects other aspects of our life. This promise is part of the covenant that He makes with us. It is important to note that He does not promise to give you exactly what you ask for, but He promises to reward you. He knows exactly what we need in each season, so our rewards are based on His perfect understanding of what will help us fulfill all that He has purposed for us to accomplish, both in this life, and in eternal life to come.

The Little Book of God's Big Promises by Dr. Elizabeth Enns

> The eternal God is your dwelling place. Underneath are the everlasting arms. He thrust out the enemy from before you.
>
> Deuteronomy 33:27 (WEB)

Week 7

When we take time to consider where we live and where we spend most of our time, we may be surprised to learn where our 'dwelling place' actually is. When you need to relax, what do you do? Where do you go? When you want to celebrate and revel in the wonders of your life, what does it look like? When you are upset, angry or afraid, where do you go? These are the questions that help us to identify our dwelling place. God has promised to be our dwelling place. In His presence he provides a place for us to be present in all situations of our life. But it is our choice if we want to dwell there. He promises to dispel the enemy but we must dwell in Him first. He has provided a safe house for us, but we have to enter it and remain there in order to be out of the enemy's reach. So my friends, today I want to encourage you to dwell in the presence of the Almighty. Be present with Him in the simple, in the triumphs, and in the trials. He desires to do life with you. So whether you need a party hall or a safe house, make His house your home.

The Little Book of God's Big Promises by Dr. Elizabeth Enns

For his anger lasts only a moment,
but his favor lasts a lifetime;
weeping may stay for the night,
but rejoicing comes in the morning.

Psalm 30:5 (NIV)

The Little Book of God's Big Promises by Dr. Elizabeth Enns

Week 8

I love the feeling of waking up in the morning after a big storm. The birds are singing and the air is fresh. I love watching the steam rise from the asphalt as the warm sun heats up the road and the shallow puddles glisten as the breeze moves across them. Mornings like that are awe-inspiring to me. There are times in our lives that we may feel God's disappointment, or even anger, but He promises us that the opportunity for His favor is so much greater. Whether good or bad, there are consequences to every action that we take. But we can take heart that our God is so rich in His love for us, that the hand that brings favor and blessings is the one that lasts. He offers us the same opportunity when it comes to our seasons of sadness, grieving and pain. The morning sun will rise and we can step out of our grief with Him and rejoice. The beauty of a new day, full of grace and wonder, awaits us after every dark night. The cold lonely darkness of the night that often accompanies fear and confusion has a time limit, and we are given the opportunity walk out of the darkness and into the glorious light. Today I encourage you to look toward the Son and receive His favor and love. Be joyful today, for He is with you and His love endures forever.

The Little Book of God's Big Promises by Dr. Elizabeth Enns

For God so loved the world that
he gave his one and only Son,
that whoever believes in him
shall not perish but have eternal life.

John 3:16 (NIV)

The Little Book of God's Big Promises by Dr. Elizabeth Enns

Week 9

We can become so complacent with the familiar. This little verse holds the greatest promise for all humanity; yet for many, it simply rolls off the tongue without a bit of weight to it. It is as if their hearts have become calloused to the actual cost and ramifications of this promise. The God of the universe, who created us and chose to give us life and sustain us each day, sacrificed His own Son. Jesus endured great suffering and took on the weight of every heinous crime for all of eternity, and was even separated from the Father so that we could be with Him for all eternity. This is huge; this promise is beyond our comprehension. All that it requires of us, is that we believe in His Son, Jesus Christ. The greatest promise available for all humanity, is the simplest to receive... all we have to do is believe.

The Little Book of God's Big Promises by Dr. Elizabeth Enns

Behold, I am with you, and will keep you, wherever you go, and will bring you again into this land. For I will not leave you, until I have done that which I have spoken of to you.

Genesis 28:15 (WEB)

The Little Book of God's Big Promises by Dr. Elizabeth Enns

Week 10

I love knowing that the Lord has spoken over my life. I find so much peace, joy and excitement in my expectation of what is yet to come. I love the assurance that the one and only living God of all creation knows me; He loves me and has an amazing purpose for my life that will bring Him glory. This is so wonderful; and what is even greater, is that it's not just for me, but for you also. God has spoken over you with an eternal destiny to bring Him glory; but there's just one thing – You have to choose. In all of His true love for us, He created free will, so that we have the choice to love Him, serve Him and walk with Him. Real love is a choice, and that is exactly what He has provided us with. Every word that the Lord has spoken over us will come to pass, if we choose Him and love Him. We will shine for the glory of the Lord as we walk with Him. Today, my friends, I want to encourage you to love the Lord with your whole being. He has purposed you for greatness, so shine and reflect His Son!

The Little Book of God's Big Promises by Dr. Elizabeth Enns

Commit to the LORD whatever you do, and he will establish your plans.

Proverbs 16:3 (NIV)

The Little Book of God's Big Promises by Dr. Elizabeth Enns

Week 11

Since the beginning of humanity, we concluded that we know better than our Creator and have some great wisdom to offer Him. We see this played out from the deception that awakened in Adam and Eve, to Cain presenting a sacrifice in direct disobedience to God's instructions; from the Tower of Babel to the Israelites rejecting God's gift of the Promised Land. Throughout the rest of history, we have proven the same truth time and time again; when we follow our own ideas and methods, our pride blocks our wisdom and leads us to destruction. God tells us in His word that we can make our own plans, but He will choose the path that is set before us. When we walk closely with the Lord, we have the opportunity to align ourselves with His ways and His plans. This allows us to know His plans and thus make His plans our plans. When we do this, He promises to establish our plans. When we fully commit every aspect of our life to the Lord, we will find that His wisdom, strategies and plans are far better than any scheme we can come up with. I want to encourage you today to take your plans and ideas, and lay them before the Lord. If they are from Him then He will bring them back around, but if He has a different direction for you, you will then be free to walk with Him. Remember, He loves you so much and His plans for you are to draw you to Himself so that you shine with brilliance for His glory.

The Little Book of God's Big Promises by Dr. Elizabeth Enns

I am the vine; you are the branches. If you remain in me and I in you, you will bear much fruit; apart from me you can do nothing.

John 15:5 (NIV)

The Little Book of God's Big Promises by Dr. Elizabeth Enns

Week 12

Somewhere deep within each of us there is this desire to do something great. We want our lives to count for something. God promises us that we will have purpose and our lives will benefit others, but it only happens with the fulfillment of a requirement. We must "remain" connected to Jesus. This is a prerequisite to the fulfillment of this promise. When we keep ourselves connected to Jesus, we receive the nourishment that we need and are able to grow in the right direction. Our purpose is to live for Christ and bring glory to the Father. We were created to be His family and provide Him with bragging rights. We long to be great in His Kingdom and we can; the invitation is there, we need only "remain". Be encouraged today to be intentional about connecting yourself to Jesus and inviting Him into your day. Better yet, commit yourself to being part of His plan and only doing what He is doing. There is much to be done, but if we are not connected to Jesus Christ as our source, then we truly can do nothing. Let's not waste our time trying to conquer the world for God on our own; many have already tried, and it just doesn't work. If He is growing and moving forward, then move forward in Him and advance the Kingdom. If He is feeding the branches that are connected to Him, then bring sustenance and nourishment to others through the Holy Spirit and the Word of God. In all things and at all times "remain" connected to Jesus and you will bear fruit, good fruit, and lots of it.

The Little Book of God's Big Promises by Dr. Elizabeth Enns

...but whoever listens to me will live in safety and be at ease, without fear of harm.

Proverbs 1:33 (NIV)

The Little Book of God's Big Promises by Dr. Elizabeth Enns

Week 13

We live in a world of uncertainty. We may think that we have secured every front and planned for every possible outcome, but at the end of the day, all of that is merely a false sense of security that quickly disappears when tragedy strikes. There is truly only one hope that we can put our trust in, and that is Almighty God. He alone is our provider and protector. He is our shield and our strength. He is the one that gives life and He is the one that sustains us. If He brought food to Elijah and caused water to come forth from a rock for all the Israelites in the desert, surely He can bring you what you need. God promises each one of us safety, peace and security when we listen to Him and follow His ways. This does not exempt us from trials and difficulties, because those will come. But the promise is that if we look to the Lord and hear His voice, He will give us exactly what we need in those moments to be victorious and triumph over the circumstances. Be encouraged today, to turn your ear to Heaven and hear what the Lord is saying. Be filled with His peace and assurance that He is with you and will never leave you. He has much to give you, you need only receive it.

The Little Book of God's Big Promises by Dr. Elizabeth Enns

> Those who trust in the LORD
> are like Mount Zion,
> which cannot be shaken
> but endures forever.

Psalm 125:1 (NIV)

Week 14

Life can be pretty tricky sometimes. It's easy to get swept into the waves that throw you back and forth and threaten to completely engulf you; but that doesn't have to be our reality. God promises that we can be like a mountain that cannot be shaken. This means that no matter how many strong storms rage around us, and massive waves crash against us, we can stand strong and not be shaken. Can you even imagine this as your reality? To look at an oncoming storm and smile, and perhaps even say under your breath, "Go ahead, make my day." It is a seemingly unbelievable reality, but it doesn't have to be. God said it and I believe it; if we trust in Him, He will make us like this mountain that is not moved. All we need to do is trust the Lord to take care of the surrounding factors that threaten our very existence. This may include our children and grandchildren, and their happiness. The list goes on and on, but it comes down to this very simple, yet not so simple, thing – trust. Can we trust? Can we trust the God who created us and knows us and loves us still? Can we trust the God who split the Red Sea and shut the mouths of lions? Can we trust the One who saved three slave boys from the hottest of fires just to remain in slavery and serve with excellence, while turning the entire culture to worship the one and only living God? Can we trust Him? I believe we can, and to be honest, the truth is that no one has been faithful or loving like He has. No one has believed in us, with all our shortcomings, like He does. Yes, I believe we can trust our God and be like that mountain… unshakable.

So today, I want to encourage you to trust Him with every aspect of your life. Allow Him to make you like a mighty mountain that stands tall and firm, not moved by the wind and waves or storms that come. Take hold of His promise and trust in Him.

The Little Book of God's Big Promises by Dr. Elizabeth Enns

> ...whoever drinks the water I give them will never thirst. Indeed, the water I give them will become in them a spring of water welling up to eternal life.
>
> John 4:14 (NIV)

The Little Book of God's Big Promises by Dr. Elizabeth Enns

Week 15

Deep within our souls we require purpose. Those who choose to live a life only for themselves, will always wrestle with an emptiness in their hearts, but those who choose to serve others, will gain a sense of purpose being fulfilled. God knows that He created us with this deep need to be part of something bigger than ourselves. So, with the promise of filling our first need – to survive, He provided the opportunity for us to fill the second need – to provide purpose. The fresh and living water that He gives us to drink, was also created to flow from us so that others may drink as well, thus giving us purpose in a much bigger plan. Offering fresh living water to the thirsty is not only life-giving for them, but also for us. Be encouraged to receive fresh living water from Jesus and allow yourself to be used by God as a spring of refreshing water for others.

The Little Book of God's Big Promises by Dr. Elizabeth Enns

He gives strength to the weary and increases the power of the weak. Even youths grow tired and weary, and young men stumble and fall; but those who hope in the LORD will renew their strength. They will soar on wings like eagles; they will run and not grow weary, they will walk and not be faint.

Isaiah 40:29-31 (NIV)

The Little Book of God's Big Promises by Dr. Elizabeth Enns

Week 16

The Lord promises us power and strength to walk, run and even soar with Him. He desires for us to be victorious. Jesus is our biggest advocate and cheers us on to succeed. God did not create us to stumble around in darkness and trip and fall over our failures. He created us to be heirs to His throne. His whole heart is for us, and He desires that we move forward in all that He has promised to us. He is glorified through our triumphant success. But like so many of our Father's promises, this is an invitation to "all who…" The promise to be strengthened in our tired, worn out moments is fulfilled when we place our hope in the Lord. He is our strength; He is our breath; He is our life. So, when we place our hope in the one who provides, then we set ourselves up to receive this amazing promise. There are many times that I find myself utterly spent. Between standing with my husband, caring for our three amazing boys, keeping my house straight-ish, and all the joyous responsibilities of church life, there are those days where I feel like I cannot take another step. But life carries on and more steps are required. It is in those moments that I go to the Lord and say, "My hope is in you. My faith is in you. My life is in you. Thank you for this moment and thank you for renewing my strength". As I thank the Lord, I begin to stir up the gift of the Spirit that is inside of me. I feel my strength being renewed and my steps that are ordered by the Lord are no longer a burden, but a source of strength. Friends, I want to encourage you to put your hope in God. He will renew your strength and give you what you need to walk, run and even soar with Him.

The Little Book of God's Big Promises by Dr. Elizabeth Enns

> Whoever fears the LORD has a secure fortress, and for their children it will be a refuge.
>
> Proverbs 14:26 (NIV)

The Little Book of God's Big Promises by Dr. Elizabeth Enns

Week 17

As a child, I remember many times that I felt afraid. Whether it was out in the wilderness or in my room, fear was a battle that I had to fight. Throughout these formative years, my parents taught me how to overcome fear and live within the secure fortress of the Lord. When we live our lives in the 'Fear of the Lord', with true reverence of His sovereignty, we position ourselves within His walls. By choosing to submit my life to the Lord, not only did I learn how to find my security in Him but, I opened the door for my own children to have a 'safe place' to grow, to live, and to advance the Kingdom of God. I encourage you to submit your entire life, your actions, your thoughts, and even your emotions to God. He will take care of you and create a place of refuge for your children as well.

The Little Book of God's Big Promises by Dr. Elizabeth Enns

You may ask me for anything in my name, and I will do it.

John 14:14 (NIV)

Week 18

Father God is so loving. He created us to be His family. He desires for us to know Him and to love Him, so He made a way for us to draw near to Him through His son, Jesus. In His fatherly love, He invites us to make our requests known to Him. Here in this verse, Jesus tells us that if we ask anything in His name, He will do it. This is sometimes difficult for us to understand, because we pray for many things and don't always see the response. There are a few truths to consider about this promise. First, is the truth that God's timing is outside of our timing, and His ways are not our ways. This tells us that the answer will come, but in God's perfect timing and perfect way so that He is glorified. The second truth to consider is that Jesus intercedes for us. He covers our prayers so that our own motives and desires of the flesh do not get in the way of our partnership with God. When we pray, Jesus presents our prayers to the Father in a way that lines up with His will. As we continue our journey of walking with the Lord, we will become more like Jesus and our prayers will line up with the will of God. Then we will see His Kingdom come on Earth as it is in Heaven.

The Little Book of God's Big Promises by Dr. Elizabeth Enns

> But you will not leave in haste or go in flight; for the LORD will go before you, the God of Israel will be your rear guard.

Isaiah 52:12 (NIV)

Week 19

Do you ever feel like it's taking so long to get to your next season? Then, when the new season finally arrives, it can feel chaotic and rushed. It's like the baby eagle that waits in the nest, longing for the day when she can soar on the heights like her mama. Then that day comes, and the mother eagle thrusts her baby out of the nest. The young, inexperienced eagle flaps her wings, panicking, fearful, and out of control, only to be rescued by her mother who brings her back up to the top to try again. We need to be encouraged to be present in the moment of where God has us, but confident that when it is time to move, Father God, in His perfect timing, will blaze the trail and have our backs all at the same time. He knows when we are ready and when He is ready to move us on. God promises us that He is ever before us while guarding us from behind. We can be reassured of our safety as we move forward in His perfect timing.

The Little Book of God's Big Promises by Dr. Elizabeth Enns

…no harm will overtake you,
no disaster will come near your tent.
For he will command his angels
concerning you to guard you
in all your ways;

Psalm 91:10-11 (NIV)

Week 20

There is something so powerful about thanking God for this promise. Even today, as I pray for a friend undergoing surgery, I find myself proclaiming these verses on her behalf. As we make these lines personal and we thank God, His wonder working power is released, and change starts to take place in the atmosphere. I often turn this into a thanksgiving prayer, saying, "God, I thank you that Your Word is absolute truth and I can put my trust in You. I thank You that You say that no harm will beat me, that no disaster will come to my home because I have made You my dwelling place. I thank You that You lead Your angels to watch over me in all that I do." I want to encourage you to proclaim these verses. Whether it is for you or for a loved one, make it personal. Make a proclamation with the Word of the Lord, and as you pair the breath of God that is within you and the Word of God, you will release His power to bring change.

The Little Book of God's Big Promises by Dr. Elizabeth Enns

Submit yourselves, then, to God. Resist the devil, and he will flee from you. Come near to God and he will come near to you.

James 4:7-8 (NIV)

Week 21

We are reminded on a regular basis that we are in the middle of a war waged against humanity. We know that in the end, the Lord has the victory, but there are many battles to be fought along the way. The enemy is also well aware that he has lost, but is determined to try to take down as many as he can. God loves us so much and desires for us to truly love Him. He promises to be near to us, and guess who can't touch you if you are near the Father? God promises us that if we say 'No' to the enemy, he has to leave. If we move close to God, then God moves closer to us. Be encouraged today to be determined to say 'No' to the enemy and all of his schemes, and 'Yes' to the Lord and His loving hand of protection.

The Little Book of God's Big Promises by Dr. Elizabeth Enns

He heals the brokenhearted and binds up their wounds.

Psalm 147:3 (NIV)

The Little Book of God's Big Promises by Dr. Elizabeth Enns

Week 22

Life can get pretty messy. I live in a house with four men. I have three amazing sons and a wonderful husband, and with that, the required cleaning load seems never-ending. The job is never finished. Just when I think that every load of laundry is folded and put away, another day of clothes are in the hamper and another meals' worth of dishes are in the washer. It's ongoing. If we, as a family, work together to pick up, clean and put things away, the job is not too overwhelming. If, however, we ignore the day-to-day effects of living, we will be overrun with filth, clutter and mess. This is a picture of our life. We can feel dirty, hurt and broken, but God, in all of His love and compassion, promises to help us with that. He will heal our brokenness and our hurts, but we have to go to Him daily. If we give all our hurts and broken pieces to Him, and receive wholeness in return, then we can take hold of this promise. I want to encourage you to be committed to allow the Lord to wash over you and heal you daily, in every season. He is the One who makes us whole.

The Little Book of God's Big Promises by Dr. Elizabeth Enns

> Before they call I will answer;
> while they are still speaking
> I will hear.

Isaiah 65:24 (NIV)

Week 23

There seems to be a special super power that moms have. This power enables them to know what their children are up to. This intuition helps moms around the globe prepare for situations before they arise, and provides the opportunity to respond well in the midst of chaos and calamity. This mystery has baffled children for generations. But behind every gift is a gift-giver. Father God, who is the perfect example of a loving parent, invented and refined this skill. He is so invested in His children that He knows what they are about to ask before the request is even made. And in His perfect timing, He sends the response, sometimes before the need is even realized. I wonder how often this happens and we don't even know it. He is so good. He loves each one of His children so completely that He promises to answer before we call out to Him and to hear us as we speak. Be encouraged to call out to Father God; He has a loving response for you.

The Little Book of God's Big Promises by Dr. Elizabeth Enns

If any of you lacks wisdom,
you should ask God, who gives
generously to all without finding fault,
and it will be given to you.

James 1:5-6 (NIV)

The Little Book of God's Big Promises by Dr. Elizabeth Enns

Week 24

I remember a professor in university challenging all our class to be 'Life-long-learners'. There was something so inspiring about this challenge; it resonated deep within my heart. Even still, almost twenty years later, it continues to echo within me. Since I was a young child I asked the Lord for His wisdom; I loved to learn and understand things that affected people and the ways of life. With learning-style, hurtles, and socioeconomic challenges, this deep hunger sometimes felt like an impossible dream; but there, in my lack, God walked with me through the valley of impossibility. I want to encourage you today that when we keep our eyes completely on Him, and do not look to the left or to the right, and when we seek Him in all things, He promises to give us His wisdom. With a complete disregard for the world's evaluation of us, Father God will be glorified as we shine with His brilliance.

The Little Book of God's Big Promises by Dr. Elizabeth Enns

No weapon formed against
you shall prosper, and every tongue
which rises against you in judgment
you shall condemn. This is the heritage
of the servants of the LORD, and their
righteousness is from Me,"
says the LORD.

Isaiah 54:17 (NKJV)

The Little Book of God's Big Promises by Dr. Elizabeth Enns

Week 25

It seems that we all face seasons where it feels like everyone is out to get us. It's like every turn we make, people and circumstances are against us. But the Lord has a promise for us to stand on in such seasons. He promises that those things that are used to take us out, will not be successful. When we walk with God, He has already decided our allotment of days. He promises that those who speak against us will receive judgment, but these promises are specific as to who will benefit. These promises are for the righteous who serve the Lord. An important factor that we should remember is that God is just; He alone is the judge and His ways are perfect. His timing in fulfilling His promise is never late. Instead, it is intentional and deliberate, in order to draw hearts to Himself. We must always forgive and bless, and let God be God. If we do, He promises us an amazing heritage in Him.

The Little Book of God's Big Promises by Dr. Elizabeth Enns

The prayer offered in faith will make the sick person well; the LORD will raise them up. If they have sinned, they will be forgiven. Therefore confess your sins to each other and pray for each other so that you may be healed. The prayer of a righteous person is powerful and effective.

James 5:15-16 (NIV)

The Little Book of God's Big Promises by Dr. Elizabeth Enns

Week 26

We live in a very broken world. All around us people are suffering and dying of illnesses. There are times when I find myself in difficult days, contending for the lives of people around me. I pray for their pain to cease and healing to come. My heart breaks as I cry out to the Lord on their behalf. I can't explain why some receive relief and healing this side of Heaven and others go on to wholeness in the presence of the Almighty. But in this journey, I hold fast to His promise; It is not some formula or recipe for success – it is The Word of God. Although the answers don't always come when we expect, and often don't look the way we imagined, they do come. He is after something so much bigger than our attention; He is after our hearts. So my friends, I want to encourage you to boldly approach the throne of God in complete humility and remind our Father of His promise. As you continue to walk with Him in righteousness and love Him wholeheartedly, He will teach you how to be powerful and effective for in His Kingdom.

The Little Book of God's Big Promises by Dr. Elizabeth Enns

In righteousness you will
be established:
tyranny will be far from you;
you will have nothing to fear.
Terror will be far removed;
it will not come near you.

Isaiah 54:14 (NIV)

The Little Book of God's Big Promises by Dr. Elizabeth Enns

Week 27

The little choices that we make each day form the beautiful tapestry that makes up our life. These choices determine the natural consequences, both desirable and not. But the Lord promises His people that if they live right, according to His ways, they will have the opportunity to be free from oppression and fear. Fear and oppression are enemies of the soul that trap and enslave people from living life abundantly in the fullness of God. It is the Lord who promotes, it is the Lord who establishes us. So, today I want to encourage you to walk in righteousness with Him so that your foot is firmly established and you can be promoted into all that the Lord intends for you.

The Little Book of God's Big Promises by Dr. Elizabeth Enns

My son, do not forget
my teaching, but keep my commands
in your heart, for they will prolong your
life many years and bring you peace
and prosperity.

Proverbs 3:1-2 (NIV)

The Little Book of God's Big Promises by Dr. Elizabeth Enns

Week 28

There are many moments when we find ourselves crying out to the Lord. The world seems to be baffled with the question of 'why' bad things happen to good people, but God's promises are true and just; He promises the opportunity for long life, peace and prosperity, so why are so many suffering? These promises are built on a covenant. If we live our lives according to the teachings of the Lord and keep His commands, then we have the opportunity to receive the fullness of these promises. The consequences that come as a result of our life choices, affect the third and forth generations, but the blessings of the Lord that come to those who walk with Him and live according to His word, go for a thousand generations. Each of these generations have the opportunity to receive these promises and live in the abundance of them. So, I encourage you today, choose to walk with the Lord and receive His promises of life, peace and prosperity.

The Little Book of God's Big Promises by Dr. Elizabeth Enns

> My Father will love them,
> and we will come to them and
> make our home with them.
>
> John 14:23 (NIV)

The Little Book of God's Big Promises by Dr. Elizabeth Enns

Week 29

On our journey through life, we are presented with this amazing opportunity to live under God's protection. We are offered His food to eat and water to drink. We are encouraged to position ourselves ever so close to the Lord, as we navigate the path, so that we can benefit from the light that He provides. I often get asked, "How do we do this?" or "What does this look like in our everyday life?" The answer is simple, yet few take hold of it. The Lord promises to love us and make His home in our hearts. That means, that He comes to us. We don't have to climb some huge mountain to get to Him; we simply invite Him in and He will come, but He will only stay if we love Him, and those who love Him follow His ways. This is not a salvation issue but an invitation to live life to the fullest. Be encouraged to invite the Lord to come and take up residence in your heart and see How it transforms your life.

The Little Book of God's Big Promises by Dr. Elizabeth Enns

> I will make them and the places surrounding my hill a blessing. I will send down showers in season; there will be showers of blessing.

Ezekiel 34:26 (NIV)

The Little Book of God's Big Promises by Dr. Elizabeth Enns

Week 30

How wonderful is the thought that we could be a blessing to others? Although this particular verse, in its context, was written for the Israelites, we can apply it to ourselves. God is a faithful covenant-keeping God, and if we love Him and walk with Him, He fulfills His covenant with us. Although there are special blessings for the Israelites, as God's chosen people, we have been grafted into an inheritance and abundant blessings. Your life will be blessed and you will prosper in the purposes of God if you walk in covenant with Him. Today, my friends, I encourage you to come into covenant with the Lord. He desires to bless you and to bless others through you. As you walk in covenant with Him, thank Him for His blessings. Thank Him for blessing others through you. Thank Him for the provisions that come in each season and see how it comes to pass.

The Little Book of God's Big Promises by Dr. Elizabeth Enns

I will heal my people and will let them enjoy abundant peace and security.

Jeremiah 33:6 (NIV)

The Little Book of God's Big Promises by Dr. Elizabeth Enns

Week 31

We have an amazing invitation to live life in "abundant peace and security" but somehow, we find ourselves wrapped up in the stress and pitfalls of anxiety and uncertainty. Sometimes our path becomes so bewildered with thorns and overgrowth, that the way through becomes invisible; we feel as though we are being entangled and swallowed up in the thorny mess of our humanity. Like the rule we were told as children, 'If you are lost, stay put until someone finds you,' it feels safer to crouch down under the weeds and thorns and stay as still as possible, hoping to be rescued. Yet, deep down we fear that we will probably be forgotten, because this predicament is entirely our fault. Although there is truth in understanding our part in creating our own mess, there is NO truth in the thought of being forgotten. There is One who also found Himself under thorns, and He knows how it feels for those thorns to press into you and pierce the skin. He knows the pain and the weight of every life choice you have made and He will never forget about you. In fact, He has barreled his way down the path swinging his axe and chopping back all the weeds and thorns. He has cleared the way for you so that you don't have to be afraid and you need only look up and take His hand. Jesus took on every burden and made a way for you to walk the path to Father God in complete security. We have this invitation to "enjoy abundant peace and security" but we must choose to look up, take His hand and walk with Him. Then, in that place, all fear, anxiety and uncertainty become very small, and are easily dismissed because you don't walk alone. I want to encourage you today, to look up and receive the hand that is extended to you. Receive Jesus Christ and walk with Him and know the peace and security that He offers.

The Little Book of God's Big Promises by Dr. Elizabeth Enns

> If you hold to my teaching,
> you are really my disciples.
> Then you will know the truth,
> and the truth will set you free.
>
> John 8:31-32 (NIV)

Week 32

We live in a society where truth seems to be difficult to uncover. From news media to government officials and everything in between, we are bombarded with opinions and accusations that are presented as truth. People throw around terms like, 'follow the science', or 'statistics tell us...' only to convince the listeners that their opinion is the one to follow.

One thing that I learned many years ago is that you can find enough 'specialists' and 'sources' to back up whatever you want to say. This dichotomy of falsehoods has just bred fear and confusion amongst people, which only leads to division and the breakdown of society. Thankfully, no matter what the news reports or what people say about it, we have a source that is absolute truth. This source founded science and created statistics, so regardless of what anyone is trying to prove, the answer is found in this source – the Word of God. The Lord promises us that He will reveal His truth to us and that we will live in freedom if we receive His teachings and live by them. Be encouraged to seek God's truth and live according to it, so that the promises of God will abound in your life.

The Little Book of God's Big Promises by Dr. Elizabeth Enns

When you pass through the waters, I will be with you; and when you pass through the rivers, they will not sweep over you. When you walk through the fire, you will not be burned; the flames will not set you ablaze.

Isaiah 43:2 (NIV)

The Little Book of God's Big Promises by Dr. Elizabeth Enns

Week 33

There are moments in our lives that we feel trapped. To go back is captivity and death but to go forward is scary and unknown. God promises us in His word that He will be with us. This means that we are not alone and don't have to figure it all out. This promise assures us that with Him, we will have the strength to make it. He promises that the elements of life that intimidate and threaten us will not harm us. I often hear people talk about their issues, baggage and scars, but what if we choose to walk so closely to God that we allow Him to straighten out our issues, cut loose our baggage and heal our scars? I have a feeling that this is what life will look like if we take hold of His promise. No matter the strength or depth of the water, God is bigger and stronger. No matter the heat of the flames, He will shield us when we walk with Him. Be encouraged to leave it all behind and cross through with the Lord.

The Little Book of God's Big Promises by Dr. Elizabeth Enns

The LORD gives strength to his people; the LORD blesses his people with peace.

Psalm 29:11 (NIV)

Week 34

Often we think of needing strength to overcome some great challenge, but what about the strength to "be still and know"? We tend to associate the need for strength with fighting, but often, in our everyday moments, we need to tap into our strength reserve to exercise self-control and take hold of the peace that has been offered to us. Father God promises us strength and peace, but we must choose to receive it and exercise it each day. If we don't practice using our strength to pursue peace within ourselves, our self-control muscles can get lazy and forget how to do this well. It requires being intentional about our thoughts, feelings and actions. Today, I encourage you to use His strength and activate the peace that God has given you.

The Little Book of God's Big Promises by Dr. Elizabeth Enns

> If you remain in me
> and my words remain in you,
> ask whatever you wish,
> and it will be done for you.

John 15:7 (NIV)

Week 35

The promises that God makes with us are so powerful. They impact us in ways that we don't even realize. At first glance, this promise can seem like an agreement between two partners. If you do something for me then I will do something for you – as if God actually needed us to do something for Him. This promise is not to mutually benefit us and God, it is to help us thrive and be successful, even when we don't realize just how much help we need. By remaining in the Lord, we connect ourselves to Him and we are fed, protected and grow. When we continue to fill our hearts and mind with His words, we are also fed, protected and continue to grow. If we are growing to be more like Jesus, then we will know what His will is, and we'll be able to partner with Him and see His power released. Be encouraged to hold on to Jesus as your source and receive the ability to live life to the fullest.

The Little Book of God's Big Promises by Dr. Elizabeth Enns

> For I am the LORD your God
> who takes hold of your right hand
> and says to you, Do not fear;
> I will help you.
>
> Isaiah 41:13 (NIV)

The Little Book of God's Big Promises by Dr. Elizabeth Enns

Week 36

Recently, I witnessed a beautiful sight that warmed my heart with such joy. I have a young neighbor that was born with an illness that brought many challenges to his development. He is the sweetest little one who we often see going for "walks" around the block, riding in his wagon. But today, I was completely surprised to see him practicing to walk down the street with the help of a walker. It was so unexpected and absolutely beautiful. In this moment, I am reminded of God's promise to help us. He knows the path that is set before us and what we need to complete it. He knows every skill and creative gift that He has put within us and He alone understands the best way to help us improve. Just like my little neighbor who needs to practice walking with the help of his walker, we too need to practice walking with the help of Father God. When we practice every day, our skills and abilities improve, and we become effective in fulfilling the purposes of God. Be encouraged today that God promises to hold your hand and help you. He wants you to know His closeness, so that you need not fear, because He has got you.

The Little Book of God's Big Promises by Dr. Elizabeth Enns

I will be with you; I will never leave you nor forsake you.

Joshua 1:5 (NIV)

Week 37

Although this promise was originally given to Joshua, we have been invited to take hold of it as well. Joshua received specific instructions from the Lord, and as he obeyed them and led the Israelites, the Lord was with Him and helped him triumph in every situation. The same is true for us. If we choose to obey the Lord and live according to His instructions, He promises to always be with us and never fail us. He will do what He said He will do. Be encouraged to be like Joshua, strong and courageous, because as you follow the Word of the Lord, He will be with you and you will not fail.

The Little Book of God's Big Promises by Dr. Elizabeth Enns

For I will give you words and wisdom that none of your adversaries will be able to resist or contradict.

Luke 21:15 (NIV)

The Little Book of God's Big Promises by Dr. Elizabeth Enns

Week 38

Do you ever have days when you face a giant and you just feel as though you will get obliterated? I have felt this way many times. I don't like to argue, I don't like when people verbally badger me; I prefer to take the road of less conflict. But, in the world that we live in, this is not always possible. That is when I find this promise so encouraging. As we walk in the ways of the Lord and grow in wisdom and understanding, He promises to give us what we need in those moments. Sometimes, I think that the Lord allows me to be speechless so that I don't make a bigger mess. When it becomes necessary, the Holy Spirit guides and directs each of us to express the matter with clarity, authority and power. So, when you see that giant coming your way, just do a little wiggle, as you hike up your waistband, take a big breath and exhale as you say, "ok God... I'm glad you're ready." Stand up tall because that giant is about to fall. Thank you, God, for sending your Holy Spirit to teach us, guide us, and dwell within us. Today, thank the Lord, that as you walk with Him, He prepares you for every moment that you face.

The Little Book of God's Big Promises by Dr. Elizabeth Enns

My eyes will be on the faithful in the land, that they may dwell with me; the one whose walk is blameless will minister to me.

Psalm 101:6 (NIV)

The Little Book of God's Big Promises by Dr. Elizabeth Enns

Week 39

God is interested in our hearts. He desires for us to know Him and to love Him. As we show ourselves faithful, He watches over us and invites us to live our lives with Him. He wants to be involved in every aspect of our day. Through our journey of walking with Him, we are transformed to be more like His son, Jesus. The blood of Jesus covers us and we become blameless before the Father. This is a beautiful and fulfilling place to be, because there, in that moment, we minister to the Father and He is glorified. I want to encourage you today to be faithful in your love for the Father. As you do, you will find a new level of fulfillment as you bless Him and minister to Him.

The Little Book of God's Big Promises by Dr. Elizabeth Enns

> The LORD himself goes before you and will be with you; he will never leave you nor forsake you. Do not be afraid; do not be discouraged.

Deuteronomy 31:8 (NIV)

Week 40

One of the best and worst things about this journey we call life is that our future is unknown. It's the worst thing because we don't know how to prepare and what to expect; we don't know how things will turn out. It's the best thing because if we knew how things would turn out, we would live life differently and then miss out on the treasures of the journey. Life is about the journey. It's about our hearts, minds and souls being so full of the beautiful love of God that everyone we cross paths with along the way is impacted by His presence in us. As we journey with the Lord, we don't need to be anxious of the unknown, but embrace it head on because God promises each of us that He goes before us. He promises to always be with us and never fail or abandon us. Be encouraged my friends, you are not alone. Don't be afraid of what you see or worried about the unknown, because the God of all creation knows you and sees you. He loves you and chooses you. He delights in you and is ever faithful.

The Little Book of God's Big Promises by Dr. Elizabeth Enns

> He will wipe every tear from their eyes. There will be no more death or mourning or crying or pain, for the old order of things has passed away.

Revelation 21:4 (NIV)

The Little Book of God's Big Promises by Dr. Elizabeth Enns

Week 41

There will come a day when the pain and trouble of this world will be no more. The Lord has given us this hope to hold on to. No matter the storm, we have been invited to keep our eyes on Him and the future that He has promised. He gives us the strength to endure and keep moving forward. The Lord has set before us a path that leads to Him, but we must not give up. We must hold on to His promises and receive His love. Be encouraged to keep your focus on Him and place your hope in His promises. All pain and sorrow will cease; death will be swallowed up in life. The old will surely pass away and His words will be fulfilled.

The Little Book of God's Big Promises by Dr. Elizabeth Enns

Make God the utmost delight and pleasure of your life, and he will provide for you what you desire most.

Psalm 37:4 (TPT)

The Little Book of God's Big Promises by Dr. Elizabeth Enns

Week 42

I love this verse. Unfortunately, it can be misunderstood and mishandled. Many people love to quote and hold on to the latter part of this promise, and then become disillusioned when they don't get what they want. The last half of the verse is contingent on the first half being fulfilled. We must make God our everything. When our whole world revolves around Him and we truly love Him, then we come to a level of joy, peace and happiness that just flows out from within us. When we reach that place in our love and adoration for the Lord, our desires line up with His heart, so that what we desire most will be Him, and He gives Himself to us in fulfillment of His covenant. I want to encourage you to embark on this amazing journey of making your love for the Father your greatest joy.

The Little Book of God's Big Promises by Dr. Elizabeth Enns

He heals the brokenhearted and binds up their wounds.

Psalm 147:3 (NIV)

Week 43

Jesus reminds us in the book of John, that here on earth, we are in for some trouble. He then reassures us to take heart, because He has overcome this world. One of the troubles that we all have to face is that of a broken heart. For some, this pain is unbearable. The loss of a loved one, whether due to death or abandonment, can cut so deep that no amount of time can truly heal. There are so many who struggle every morning to face yet another day with this burden. The anguish of a broken heart can weigh so heavy, but it doesn't have to stay forever. God, in all of His love and compassion, extended an opportunity for each one of us to rise out of this pain and walk in healing and wholeness. He is the one who heals our hearts and wraps us up so that we can be restored and healed. This happens as we spend time with Him, allowing His grace and love to wash over us. If you are hurting, I encourage you to allow the love of our Father to surround you and bring healing to your heart. He desires for you to be whole.

The Little Book of God's Big Promises by Dr. Elizabeth Enns

Ask and it will be given to you;
seek and you will find;
knock and the door will be
opened to you.

Matthew 7:7-8 (NIV)

Week 44

Hidden deep within the human condition is the need for purpose. If everything in life is simply available at our fingertips, we never reap the benefits of being strengthened. Instead, we become weak and entitled. God knows that He created us for His glory, and He desires for us to be the bride for His Son. He doesn't want us to be weak and entitled, but rather a strong, victorious bride of valor. He promises that we will receive what we ask for, and find what we look for, but it requires action on our part. We have to put forth the effort of asking and looking. In order to ask someone for something, you must be in their presence. Father God is generous and does not withhold any good thing from those who love Him, but He is waiting for us to come to Him and spend time in His presence to receive what He has for us.

The Little Book of God's Big Promises by Dr. Elizabeth Enns

Cast your cares on the LORD
and he will sustain you;
he will never let
the righteous be shaken.

Psalm 55:22 (NIV)

The Little Book of God's Big Promises by Dr. Elizabeth Enns

Week 45

There are days when we are surprised and taken off guard. We can feel shaken up, knocked down or out of place. God promises us that if we throw all our concerns on Him, then He will keep us safe. If we walk with Him in righteousness, nothing can move us. God can move us and we can move ourselves, but that's it. If we position ourselves in His hand, no one can remove us. So, then we must come back to the question of why we, as children of God, feel worried or afraid? If He's the one holding us, then we have nothing to fear. I want to encourage you today to be intentional about giving every care and concern to the Father and leave it with Him. Don't pick it back up. If you desire to be sustained and carried by the Lord, then give it all to Him. Trust Him, He cares for you; you don't need those worries anyway.

The Little Book of God's Big Promises by Dr. Elizabeth Enns

…if you faithfully obey the commands I am giving you today–to love the LORD your God and to serve him with all your heart and with all your soul–then I will send rain on your land in its season, both autumn and spring rains, so that you may gather in your grain, new wine and olive oil. I will provide grass in the fields for your cattle, and you will eat and be satisfied.

Deuteronomy 11:13-15 (NIV)

Week 46

It seems as though many just want the harvest without the rain, and even if they recognize the blessings of the rain, they forget about the 'if'. God promises us the opportunity for provisions to fully meet our needs but it comes with a condition – the 'IF' factor. If we are intentional about learning what God has commanded us to do, and if we are faithful to actually obey His instructions, then we can stand on this promise of provision. We can fully trust in the fulfillment of this promise when we truly LOVE God. It's easy to say that we love God but what is God's love language? God knows that we love Him when we live according to His Word. It's when we follow His commands and not live according to our desires and feelings. 'What you feel like doing' and 'what you want to do' really don't have a place in the 'IF' factor, because our flesh will fail us every time. God wants us to put aside our fleshly desires and just live for Him. Today, I encourage you to be intentional about knowing God's way and following it. He will not mislead you; in fact, He will direct you in the way everlasting, in life abundantly. On that journey, you will find His promises of provision fulfilled.

The Little Book of God's Big Promises by Dr. Elizabeth Enns

If you believe, you will receive whatever you ask for in prayer.

Matthew 21:22 (NIV)

Week 47

God's Word is true, and I know with full confidence that we can put our trust in Him. The Word tells us in II Corinthians that all of God's promises are yes and amen. Jesus tells us that if we believe, then we will receive what we ask for in His name. These seem like tricky statements, because the world is full of people who asked God for something and have yet to see the fulfillment of it. What do we do with this? How do we explain and come to terms with this? This is part of our faith journey with the Lord, and in it there are things that we will not fully understand this side of Heaven. In Hebrews 11:39-40 we can read about the fathers and mothers of the faith, when it says, "These were all commended for their faith, yet none of them received what had been promised, since God had planned something better for us so that only together with us would they be made perfect." So, in this promise, we must hold on to the truth that God loves us and has something even greater in store. On our faith journey, we learn how to trust Him and His unconditional love for us; He has amazing things prepared for us.

The Little Book of God's Big Promises by Dr. Elizabeth Enns

He will cover you with his feathers,and under his wings you will find refuge; his faithfulness will be your shield and rampart.

Psalm 91:4 (NIV)

Week 48

The Lord is so gracious in how He cares for us and protects us. There are times when we cry out to the Lord, asking Him why we are not protected in difficult times. There are so many people that find themselves rejecting God because they were not protected and felt abandoned. These are realities that many face, but it is important that we look at the whole promise. God will cover us, but we have to position ourselves under His covering. Within the illustration of being covered by His wings, it is implied that we must be close to His heart. His wings are not like an umbrella that we just take with us wherever we go. We must run to Him, get close to His heart and hide ourselves under His covering. We can't run off doing our own thing, choosing our own path, and then expect to be covered. We must be intentional about remaining so close to Him in every season.

The Little Book of God's Big Promises by Dr. Elizabeth Enns

The LORD is good,
a refuge in times of trouble.
He cares for those who trust in him

Nahum 1:7 (NIV)

The Little Book of God's Big Promises by Dr. Elizabeth Enns

Week 49

It is so easy to say that we love God and that we trust God, but we can't truly know for sure until the flood waters are rising and there is no boat in sight. If we truly trust Him, then how we respond in times of such difficulty will show us where we stand. The Lord is good, He is loving, and He cares for us deeper than we can understand. The troubles and trials that we face are to test and strengthen us. They are not to show God what we are made of... because He already knows. They are to show us what we are made of and what areas need to be strengthened. Father God is after our hearts; He has such an amazing purpose for us but we must be ready. We must learn how to walk in full trust, knowing that He is with us, that He loves us, and that He will see us through. Be encouraged today to put your trust – your whole trust – in Him. If He doesn't send a boat, perhaps it is because He wants to teach you to swim.

The Little Book of God's Big Promises by Dr. Elizabeth Enns

Let us not become weary in doing good, for at the proper time we will reap a harvest if we do not give up.

Galatians 6:9

The Little Book of God's Big Promises by Dr. Elizabeth Enns

Week 50

Mother Theresa once said, "I do not pray for success, I ask only for faithfulness." It is all too easy to be disheartened by not seeing the results that we desire. When things are not looking the way that we expected them to, we can allow our fatigue to dictate our outcome. We are reminded in scripture to deny ourselves and live our days fully for the Lord. This means that even if it doesn't look the way that we thought it should, if God tells us to do it, we need to be faithful and keep at it. Only God knows what is happening to the seed below the surface of the soil. God knows how much time and warm sun is required; He knows how much spring rain will be enough for that seed to sprout up out of the soil. Be encouraged today to shake yourself off and keep at it. Don't get worn out from being the hands and feet of Jesus. Be renewed and transformed; keep going, for the Lord has much love for us to spread.

The Little Book of God's Big Promises by Dr. Elizabeth Enns

Be strong and courageous, and do the work. Do not be afraid or discouraged, for the LORD God, my God, is with you. He will not fail you or forsake you until all the work for the service of the temple of the LORD is finished.

1 Chronicles 28:20 (NIV)

Week 51

Do you ever feel that there is a new challenge waiting for you around every corner? Do you feel like these challenges are usually way bigger than what you can handle? Well I have good news for you – they ARE bigger than you can handle. That is probably because there are always new challenges bigger than you can handle. God desires to mold us, stretch us and transform us, and He does that by choosing assignments that are bigger than our capabilities. But here's the key – He never intended for you to do it alone. He desires for us to partner with Him. He does all the heavy lifting. We just have to remember to remain in Him and do what He does, because with God all things are possible (Mt.19.26). So today, I encourage you to "Be strong and courageous" and look that challenge right in the face and laugh, for with Almighty God by your side, you shall not fail.

The Little Book of God's Big Promises by Dr. Elizabeth Enns

…in all these things we are more than conquerors through him who loved us. For I am convinced that neither death nor life, neither angels nor demons, neither the present nor the future, nor any powers, neither height nor depth, nor anything else in all creation, will be able to separate us from the love of God that is in Christ Jesus our LORD.

Romans 8:37-39 (NIV)

The Little Book of God's Big Promises by Dr. Elizabeth Enns

Week 52

In this world of uncertainty, many lose sight of the steadfast certainty of God. God is not fickle or tumultuous like our world is; He is unmovable, He is all knowing, He is love. No power is greater than God and His love for you. No one can pull you out of His hand. You need not fear the enemy that comes to destroy, because as long as you place yourself in the hand of God, the Devil cannot have you. We are promised that no one can separate us from the love of God. Even if we walk away, God is still love. The Father created you to be His child, and His outrageous love for you cannot be measured by human understanding. He loves you completely. Be encouraged today to receive His all-inhabiting love and take your place in the palm of His hand.

www.ingramcontent.com/pod-product-compliance
Lightning Source LLC
Chambersburg PA
CBHW071007080526
44587CB00015B/2377